Hi, My Name Is...

Survival Guide for a Successful Career Path Transition

by Desha "DrDesha" Elliott

B.O.S.S. Publishing
Atlanta, GA

B.O.S.S.
Publishing

Copyright

Hi, My Name Is... Survival Guide for a Successful Career Path Transition
A B.O.S.S. Book

Published by
B.O.S.S. Publishing, a subsidiary of Clay & Clay, LLC.
Atlanta, Georgia

All Rights Reserved.
Copyright © 2015 by Desha "DrDesha" Elliott
Cover Design by Emmanuel Johnson
Book Design by Andrea Paul

Library of Congress Control Number Applied for.

B.O.S.S. Publishing and the book servicemark are registered trademarks of Clay & Clay, LLC.

ISBN-13: 978-0-9863559-9-8

Printed in the United States of America

www.boss-publishing.com

10 9 8 7 6 5 4 3 2 1

Hi, My Name Is...

Survival Guide For A Successful Career Path Transition

Desha "DrDesha" Elliott

Contents

Hi, My Name Is...   9
Introduction

Building Your Brand, Building You   10
Chapter 1

The Power of Social Media   14
Chapter 2

The Art of Networking   26
Chapter 3

The Meaning of Exposure   37
Chapter 4

The Lesson of Spending Wisely   43
Chapter 5

Conclusion   49

Glossary   51

Hi, My Name Is...

Before you give up on being an entrepreneur, let this guide remedy your entrepreneurial woes. Before you deny your desire to make a career change, continue reading. If you believe in your product and you believe in yourself, let's get you back on track with where you want to be.

By sharing my mistakes and the lessons I've learned, you will get a clear understanding of how you should focus your energy and time on strategies that will take your you, your business, and your career to the next level. Success is at your fingertips... take advantage of the knowledge you are holding in your hand.

This book is an easy how-to guide to help you market your passions, develop your brand, and meet the right kinds of people to help you succeed. It can become as easy as saying "Hi."

Chapter 1

Building Your Brand, Building You

Pretending to stand behind a product or values that I wouldn't normally stand by.

In an attempt to try something new, I figured I would pitch the latest and greatest in juicing technologies. I was under pressure by the person who brought me into this industry because their reputation depended on my success. "This is an exciting change in your career path! The person who signed me on works for themselves and has lots of money and time to go on extravagant vacations!" This is what my higher up said to reaffirm my choice in joining their team. My success with this product was determined by how many people would buy into my presentation and pay for regular juicing packages. I was told to call everyone in my phone, regardless of whether I believed they had interest or the ability to pay for my product or be considered to work under me. I caught myself in mid-presentation, apologizing for *wasting other's time and becoming furious for wasting my time and resources for a product and business model I didn't trust.*

Your success in any industry will be contingent on you, your brand, and how much people are able to invest into your brand, whether with time or resources. Your brand is your stamp on the world that showcases your talents, beliefs, and accomplishments. Your brand's success depends on you knowing the answers to:

- Who are you?
- What makes you unique?
- What are your passions?
- What do you do exceptionally well that others commend you for?
- Why should people come to you for what you do well?
- What are your values and principles?
- What kind of legacy do you want to leave behind?

When you can truthfully answer these questions, you will be able to tell others about your brand and align yourself with those who can help you stay authentic to your brand.

Chapter 1

Authenticity is essential because dishonesty fosters mistrust. If people cannot trust you, they will not invest in you. When you are being disingenuous with what you believe, while you may be able to deceive yourself for some time, you are going to get to a point when your true self can no longer stay hidden.

My mistake in wanting to sell to others and promote a product I didn't truly support ended up showing in my actions, doubts, and uncertainty within my pitch. Initially, I may have been able to pretend the product was as incredible as sliced bread, but my work ethic and my attitude became lethargic. The other matter to consider is that I was put into a position to where I had to inform people in my circle that I was affiliated with this product, that this product generated my team and I lots of income, and that they should come work under me selling this product. That was a lie that I couldn't even grasp.

Convincing people that they should pay you for your service or product because of the benefits it brings to them as a customer is a never-ending process. If you are misleading your clients about the benefits of your service or product, those lies can influence your customer's perception about your product, and ultimately, your brand and how others perceive you.

Chapter 2

The Power of Social Media

Being selfish with my social media engagement.

Allured by Facebook and Twitter telling me to try out their advertising services to effectively reach new clients, I decided to give it a try. I came up with a few ads asking customers to "buy now" and "save on this." No one actually purchased anything from me as a result of my paid advertising. All I had was research saying who my product would appeal to. I was truly disheartened.

Social media is a powerful marketing tool that can help you leave a branding footprint on the internet. Like any other tool, you need to know how to properly use social media. This way, it can do the most for you and your brand. Do you hammer screws? No! You use a screwdriver for screws, you use a hammer for nails. This same premise is how you should utilize social media.

Social media is an extension of yourself and your brand onto the internet. While there is much to be gained from face to face contact, those who have never met you or those who have become your newest followers can truly get a feel for your brand, what you stand for, and what you promote. Social media is also a great way to find people you need to connect with, as well as help you find individuals you wish to keep in touch with so you may keep the relationship open.

With plenty of social media platforms and users into the billions, there are so many opportunities to connect with those who can help you achieve your dreams. I will focus on a few main social media sites just so you can get a general understanding of their purpose and use each of these sites.

Facebook

Even though this platform was created to keep in touch with your college buddies, it soon expanded to allow you to stay in touch with up to 5,000 friends and have an unlimited number of "likes." Depending on your motives, you can create an additional business page to promote your business and share content relevant to your industry. You can invite your current friend base to stay up to date on your successes by having them "like" your business page. This is an easy way to grow your email/ contact list.

Facebook also has an instant messaging component that allows you to privately contact individuals on your friend list. Please be wary of instant messages that are from people you don't know, as well as messages that contain random links or weird greetings. Sometimes this may be spam or those looking to scam you. Also, be considerate of other's preferences. If you want to send them a flier or post information about your product or event, ask them beforehand.

Google+

With *Google+*, you can easily sort individuals based on their relationship to you (friends, family, acquaintance, advertiser, clients, etc). Once you are connected with an individual, what they post on their *Google+* will come down in a feed similar to *Facebook*'s homepage. You can share the content, like it, or even comment on it! Again, just like *Facebook,* it will remind you of special occasions that happen in the lives of those you let in your circle.

Twitter

Want to express yourself in less characters to a wider range of audiences? Then *Twitter* is the place for you. In 140 characters or less, you can express an opinion, solve a problem, or reach out to a customer. By developing enough of a following and gaining interest in your posts, you will see an increase of retweets, where the message is reposted on a follower's timeline for their network of people to see it, and favorites, where people can save your tweet to show support of your post or for later viewing.

LinkedIn

LinkedIn is an amazing professional platform that you can use to connect with those who are looking to work with you/hire you. With the information you put into this site to build your page, it is formatted in an easy to read résumé style profile. You can even download this information onto a PDF and submit is as a résumé for others to view.

You can input jobs, education, achievements, and referrals. This site is also amazing for the business related updates and stories you can post, as well as the reminders they give you about the successes and achievements of your connections. Keep your connection going past a simple introduction by congratulating them on their promotion or that you wish them an awesome work anniversary.

Instagram, Pinterest, Vine, Ustream, and Youtube

I decided to group these services together because these platforms are more visual compared to the prior platforms. Visuals help to personify and give color to your brand. Capturing captivating, candid shots of your business activities and interactions, engaging other companies you support, and interacting with clients help to bring familiarity and authenticity to your image. How difficult would it be for me to call myself a chef if you've never seen a picture of my food, my process in the kitchen, or my food service skills? The average person would question your skills because of your lack of visualizations.

Instagram is really amazing for helping you visually connect with followers and it is easy to utilize because you just need to capture a picture or 15 second video that can summarize the moment you want to share with other people. Capture your interaction with other people and ask them for their *Instagram/ Facebook/ Twitter* names to connect with them and connect them with your audience.

Pinterest can be really beneficial for visual research, for sharing your likes with others, and for creating an online vision board. You can share your *Pinterest* with others, create specific lists for each of your interests, or keep your "boards" private for when you are gathering ideas for your business. As a marketing tool, if your business has great visuals, embedding a link inside the post for people to further connect with you is a must do.

Vine is something that has been used primarily for entertainment purposes and great for showcasing comedians and other talent. With Vine, you upload a 6 second video that would allow for looping. This is great if you want to introduce a new product in a creative brief video. Here, the more creative the presentation to utilize the looping feature, the better.

UStream has an ability for you to do a real time, live video stream with those who follow your channel. You can respond to their inquires or chat in real time and showcase. This is a great platform if you are looking to engage your audience on a more personable level.

Youtube offers a way to post videos you have pre-recorded and others can watch it as many times as they want. Musicians, actors, chefs, and many others have garnered attention from their *Youtube* channels and have been able to launch their careers all because they showcased their talents on this platform. Recently, *Youtube* has launched their own live video feature in conjunction with *Google+* and *Google Hangouts*, much like *UStream*. You will have to decide which platform is best for your business and audience.

Blogging

I was able to be viewed as an expert on my blog, RealtimeDrD. I used this blog mainly as a way to give free promotion for independent artists and smaller businesses. You can create a blog to give your expert insight about your passions and topics revolving around your brand. *Blogger, Tumblr,* and *Wordpress* have built in space to express your thoughts on a subject matter for free.

Hashtag and Selfie Power

Hashtags are miniature stamps used to describe what it is you are posting. You simply put the "#" symbol with a word or phrase immediately next to it (eliminating spaces in-between words). These hashtags help when people are searching for your posts, their interests, or expert opinion on the internet. If you put *#cheflife* on your social media posts, photos, and videos, when someone searches your hashtag in the search engine, your #cheflife posts have left a stamp on the internet and others have a chance to find you. The more creative or more consistent your hashtags, the more you will generate a lasting internet presence.

Selfies are pictures that you have taken of yourself. While it may seem as if the masses use this as an opportunity to post their look for the day, selfies can be a great marketing and networking tool, if done properly. When you meet someone new, or when you are working on a project for your business, take a selfie. You never know how much attention you may draw to your product and to your work ethic by humanizing your work.

Social Media Disclaimers

As mentioned at the onset of the chapter, social media is a tool that works best when used properly. Used improperly, it can have negative effects that may be hard to get rid of. For example, let's say that you had an unsatisfied customer who had just recently purchased one of your latest pieces. This one person can go on the internet and blast out a negative review that will be available for the whole wide web to see. How you handle that comment on social media will have a bearing on how potential clients view you, your business, and your brand. This is your opportunity to show new and existing customers that you take all complaints seriously and will attempt to make the situation better. If you do not respond or take a negative approach to the post, you will turn away potential customers because they will feel like they cannot trust you. Remember if you can't be trusted, others will not invest in you. Use this moment as a Public Relations opportunity to showcase your brand in the best possible light to attract new and returning clients.

Another disclaimer when using social media is to be mindful in terms of the visualizations you may post. If you are desiring an ideal position in an accounting firm, yet your posts display you as an angry, irresponsible, drunken individual, that firm has a right to refuse you as a candidate. If your social media image contradicts what the company stands for, when they go to research your background (social media is public, so yes, that is a part of your background check) and your negative images pop up, they will refuse to hire you. If you can't be trusted, others will not invest in you and the goals of your brand.

Lastly, understand that you will not go very far with having a network you cannot actively depend on, especially if you only use social media as a platform to share your promotions. If you are guilty of having a weak social media network, then you might as well put your promotions on highway billboards. Although, that billboard more than likely wouldn't generate many responses or opportunities to engage and build rapport with your customers as quickly as social media, That advertisment will get a few individuals through your door or to your website. But, it all means nothing without interaction and engagement.

You wouldn't like it if you met someone and they never bothered to listen to what you had to say, but they continued to promote their interests. This can be the case with social media, as well. Many businesses that I have worked with say that they paid for ads on social media, but do not see how it helped their business. When you pay for an ad, you are paying for the number of people you can reach that match the specifications of your target audience. You are paying to post and for the audience reach. What will come immediately as a result of paying for this service, is the increase in the amount of people that saw your ad. However, without engagement, without customers being compelled or drawn in by your advertisement, paying for posts will not guarantee a return in dollars. It is up to you to keep engaging and following up with the audience that is exposed to your product. A consumer may have to see your products/services three more times before they remember what it is and establish their need for it. Therefore, seeing your social media as something that has to be built and properly managed will help you realize how to effectively use social media as a tool for your brand.

Chapter 2

Social media isn't going to be effective if you are constantly posting advertisements. You need to build your followers and engage with them regularly. Converse with your current and potential followers about their thoughts and opinions on your industry and your product. Even take the time to like and share appropriate posts created by your followers. There are billions of users on these platforms and there is a way for a small percentage of those to become aware of you and your services.

Chapter 3

The Art of Networking

Believing that giving away and obtaining the most business cards means that you made meaningful connections.

Merely receiving and offering a plethora of business cards is as bad as attending an event where I didn't speak to anyone and I merely positioned myself as a wallflower.

I signed up to attend two networking sessions in one week. At one session, I passed out my card to everyone in sight. I collected quite a few business cards, but I never really spoke to anyone about what they did; I just said a quick greeting and moved on to the next individual. I didn't receive any follow up contact from anyone I met that night, just a few general business spam emails. At my networking event later that week, I stood against the wall all night. I observed a few people, even nodded my head at others that walked by. I didn't introduce myself to a single person.

If you had to depend on the people in your circle, in your network to help you get your next job, house, or sound advice about your career path, could you do it? Could you do it effectively? Building a solid network where there is an interchange of opportunities among you and your network is one of the main reasons why networking is key. My network has enabled me to live in the city I wanted to live in doing the work I love to do. How beneficial is your network to you? How do you build up your network?

Networking can occur anywhere. While there are specialized networking events (that you could find easily through *Meetup*), be ready to network anywhere at any time. You never know who you may meet standing in line at the grocery store, at the doctor's office, or in a diner. Being ready means that you can accurately convey who you are, what you do, or what are trying to achieve in less than fifteen seconds. Networking also requires you to have a way for someone to follow up with you. This could be with a business card, website, text message, or your social media handles.

To Be or Not To Be Outgoing

To network with someone, there has to be a form of exchanged dialogue. While some of your dialogue may be over email or phone, a lot can be accomplished in person. You know that person in the room who is animated, captivating, boisterous, and may have a crowd of people around them? This person is considered to be outgoing. However, if you are not this person, it is not the end of the world. You can still be effective in face to face settings. There are some people who simply love the energy they get from interacting with people and dislike spending time alone. Whereas, introverted people would prefer to be by themselves and actually become drained by social interactions.

Bill Gates, Rosa Parks and Elton John are introverted people, yet they have achieved huge milestones in their lives and careers. More often than not, your actions and not what you say carry more weight in networking. We will examine some exercises that will help you overcome your shyness just enough to connect with individuals and leave a lasting impression.

Networking Exercises

Networking at specialized networking events or in bigger arenas (conventions or galas) can be intimidating and overwhelming for some. Here are some exercises that can help you make the most of those occasions:

- Have knowledge of the event and who may be possibly in attendance.

You can research the type of event it is by looking it up online, viewing any pictures associated with the event, or by even reaching out to the coordinator and asking who will be in attendance. Reaching out to the coordinator or the person who invited you also creates a safety point for you since they will know you at the party and can help you meet the next person.

- Go and meet three to five people you do not know well.

It is easy to stay with someone we know and talk with them all night. But, you already know this person. It doesn't cost you anything to politely introduce yourself to someone and simply ask them how they are associated with the event. If you want to stay connected with that individual, be prepared to ask them how you may follow up with them. It's okay to meet people you may never have an immediate connection with or who you may not see again. Just getting the hang of introducing yourself and knowing how to interact is what you want to achieve. You never know where one introduction and conversation may lead to.

- Practice the kinds of conversations you want to have beforehand.

Imagine meeting someone and you don't have anything in common. Now, imagine you meet a person who is in a field you are looking to get into. Building that confidence and putting yourself in an interactive mind frame at home or in the car on the way there helps you prepare for the moment. So, when that moment actually happens, you will be less likely to freeze up and stumble over your words.

Even though my field has me speaking to many different people all of the time, it makes me energized and drained at the same time. Networking reminds me of going for a run. Before you run, you warm up and stretch. I regularly think about the kind of conversations I will encounter with people and practice my responses. Sometimes I even pray, meditate, or do jumping jacks to increase my endorphins and put myself in ready mode. Then, I give myself an assignment, because I am a goal-driven person. Can I meet two new people today? Can I meet someone who works with nonprofits? Sometimes, I network not only for myself but for others I know. A lot of times, people ask me if I know an expert in a particular field or who is hiring, and it is because of research and networking I am privy to this information. At times, I feel more comfortable just being off in the corner with a book in my hand. However, putting myself in readiness mode gets me focused on my networking tasks. Then, oddly enough once I get going, it's almost like a runner's high, where you get your second burst of energy. I feel energized from continuously moving and interacting.

Rules of Engagement

Depending on your culture, become familiar with the ways that you greet people. Normally, most cultures have very specific ways to greet others depending on if they are of the opposite sex and if they are older/younger than you. Once you have established and exchanged the proper greeting, be observant and listen with your eyes, as well as your ears. Are they wearing an emblem that represents something they stand for? Is their body language suggesting that they are in a hurry or disinterested? Looking out for these subtle clues helps you to better assess the person you are engaging with, as well as help you stay focused on your task at hand, which is to network.

You also want to show genuine interest in your interaction. Even if you have to excuse yourself away from the situation, do so politely. This person may or may not hold one of the keys to your success, so you could at least be cordial and considerate while you converse with them. This allows you to be prepared to follow up with them afterwards. Taking the time to do so will show your professionalism and also help the other person remember who you are and willingly share if they know of a person or opportunity that can benefit you. Be prepared to follow up more than once (in a reasonable amount of time–two days to a week if it is a potential client or two weeks to a month if a potential connection) to maintain the relationship.

If you are in an event where there is alcohol or other substances that impair human judgment, be cautious when interacting with those who are using those items. Also, be careful of your own intake of these items. Your focus is to speak to others about your brand and making connections. Your conduct will definitely have an affect on whether people will want to stay connected with you. If you are speaking to someone who is under the influence, they may not be of the right mind at that time to make wise decisions or even remember meeting you.

The Follow Up

Following up with the connections you meet is beneficial because you never know how meeting that person will change your circumstances. Ask your new connect the best way to reach out to them. Did they give you a business card? Can you find them on *LinkedIn*? If they are someone you want to really maintain the conversation with, make sure to look for their achievements so you can congratulate them. You could support their next appearance, buy their book, or even send them an interesting article you read based on the conversation that you had.

I met a college professor at a recent conference I went to. We stumbled upon the conversation of good books to read so I told her about the _Slight Edge_ by Jeff Olsen. Next thing I knew, she read and loved the book and made it a mandatory reading for her class! There is a whole classroom full of young adults who will look at their work ethic and their finances in a new way all because I took the time to show personal interest in this teacher and had a meaningful connection.

If you have problems speaking to strangers, if you have trouble marketing yourself, or if you want to be put in a position where you will be held accountable for allowing your skills to be pushed to the next level, exposing yourself to events and workshops will be beneficial for your success. I still get so many butterflies when I have to go out and speak to others, and at times, even telling people about myself can even take a lot of strength. To push myself to greatness, I put myself in situations where I have to talk to people or I have to get out of my comfort zone in order to grow.

Collecting massive amounts of cards without any purpose is as meaningful as Monopoly Money is to the economy. A contact is only as powerful as the next steps you are able to take with the connection. If you are unable to confidently present what you or your business is about, take the time to practice.

When going to networking events (whether small or large), do research about who will be in attendance and know who you want to specifically reach. Be able to present a mutual benefit to the other person to give them a reason to stay in touch with you.

Chapter 4

The Meaning of Exposure

Thinking that once I said I had a certain product or skill people would automatically want to work with me.

When I decided to transition out of working at a government office to work more with marketing, I told my family and friends. While my decision was met with dismay, no one was giving me any real advice about where to go or what to do next. Even when meeting new people, I would tell them my latest venture, I had to counter their confusion to end the conversation with them saying, "okay" or "best of luck to you." Why weren't people lining up to work with me?

From working as a model to working in the music industry, *exposure* was a common word everyone used. If you weren't famous yet, it was because you didn't have enough "*exposure.*" If you didn't have enough talent in your craft, it was because you lacked the "*exposure*" to the right teachings. Exposure is also what is necessary in order for you to achieve your dreams. How will we know about your products/services if we haven't been exposed to your end results? How will you meet those necessary for your network if you are not exposed to the right environments to meet them?

Exposure can come in the form of an event, such as a volunteer event or mixer. It may even be a class or workshop that you take in order to become better at your craft. I will further show how to take advantage of these exposure situations.

Depending on your skills, there are events you can sign up for as a vendor, to volunteer, or to attend that will allow you to expose your talents and meet people to add to your circles. Do you have the latest technology invention? Sign up for competitions or to be a vendor at a technology event to showcase your product. Is there a convention that has your favorite leader or a company that you want to build a connection with? If you are not able to purchase tickets to attend the event, offer to volunteer or work the event. Once you get your foot in the door, align yourself with both those people whom you need to meet and others in the events, as well. I especially want to highlight volunteering. Whether you are volunteering for a charitable cause or you are volunteering to get inside an event of your interest, take advantage of getting to know the people who are behind the event and even those you are volunteering with.

Sometimes I will volunteer my time, or sign up to be involved with a program to sharpen my skills, as well as expand my network. I sign up to walk in fashion shows every year, not necessarily because I want to be a top model, but because I want to meet people who have other talents and causes they are passionate for. After the event, we end up running into each other or helping each other in one way or another. There is a person in my network that I have worked with for over 6 years and I met this person because of my involvement in a fashion show.

I am an advocate of education in all forms and I recommend taking courses, classes, or going to workshops to help improve your craft. The people who run those classes and workshops can really help push you to the next level in your career and you can even develop great relationships with the attendees of those courses. However, like with anything, please do your research. Research the credibility of the instructors, the benefits of the course to your career, and the results of those who have taken the course. No one is going to care more about the advancement of your career than yourself. There are some unscrupulous individuals who hold workshops, host opportunities, or have other products that they want you to invest in that are not worth your time and money. Stay focused and do not let anyone take one dime from you until you can verify their validity and credibility.

Chapter 4

When making a change in your career or pursuing a new business venture, you will have to immerse yourself in that industry or that industry's dealings so you can grow within that line of work. Your connections and leads will increase by being present at relevant events and workshops. It is unreasonable to think that people will automatically know who can point you in the right direction if you haven't made productive steps toward bringing awareness to your venture.

Chapter 5

The Lesson of Spending Wisely

Spending an unreasonable amount of money on ineffective strategies.

In an attempt to promote my latest acquired skill, I paid money to advertise my skills and contact info on billboards. I also hired five to seven people I had just met to be my promotional team. My billboards generated phone calls but those calls weren't for my business. My promotional team scared customers away and was combative when I would inquire about their supposed marketing efforts.

Often times, I hear people say that they are limited on their money and that marketing can be pricey. Your success is an investment, and even if it's not money, then it's time. How much does your success mean to you?

Money Truths
How much does it cost to take a picture of

someone? How much does it cost for you to find the nearest networking event or class needed to boost your career? How much does it cost to say "Hi"? Everything I mentioned can be achieved in the range of $0 to $1500 depending on your location, your connection, and the expertise of those you may hire to help you complete these tasks. While paying for outside help to market can become pricey, I will highlight what you can do by yourself and with the least amount of money. Here are a few less-than-one-hundred-dollar ideas to help build your brand and market your career:

- **_Marketing Follow-Up Tools:_** You can create business cards to pass out to individuals for less than $50. You can create a simple website for less than $50 via Wordpress or Wix. Skype is an inexpensive way to communicate and market your services that you want your client to sign up for. It is also used for meetings and job interviews.

- **_Social Media:_** Social media sites are free to sign up to and use. You can use a camera phone to take pictures and record your visual branding moments. Want a logo or a neat animated way to showcase your work? Look at sites like Fiverr.com to help you with creating your ideas from $5-$25. You can even do cross promotion with another company or organization. See if they would promote you or your product if you agree to have a link or their logo on your site as well.

- **_Membership:_** Join clubs and groups that are related to your field. Do you want to be in human resources? One of the best organizations to join is the *Society for Human Resource Management*. Most organizations have different chapters depending on your location. They even have opportunities to bring it to your town if there is no chapter nearby. Membership fees vary and may be annual.

- **_Blogging:_** Earlier, we established that blogs can be used to give your advice on a subject. To create these blogs, *Blogger*, *Wordpress*, and *Tumblr* are free as long as you set up a profile through the respective site.

- **_Seek out opportunities:_** Look in your local newspaper for articles and advertisements that expose you to opportunities or individuals you may want to connect with. *Craigslist* is an online classifieds message board and website. While there are many questionable posts on this site, those that are written professionally and provide great detail and contact information for the company and event are the ones you should reach out to with your interest. I would also suggest using sites like *Meetup* that pair you with groups based on your interests. You'd be surprised at the amount of groups in your community! *Meetups* make it easier to strike up a conversation because you will at least have a mutual interest in being at the event with the individual you are speaking with. Within the *Meetup* website, you are able to message attendees beforehand so you can build a rapport with someone and meet them at the event.

- **_Hire personnel:_** If you need outside marketing help, there may be students at a nearby college that you can reach out to who can help you build your brand while they gain exposure and build their resume. They can assist you with your marketing needs for low costs.

No matter if you employ a student or a professional, make sure to do your research and obtain more than one quote for the services you want. Make sure that whomever you choose to do your marketing, that you have a written contract or *Memorandum of Understanding* that specifies what they will do, the length of their service period, a breakdown of costs, and a clause that covers if you are not satisfied with their work. There are many advantages to hiring an expert to perform and manage your marketing material, but make sure you hire someone who is going to give your brand the work and professionalism that you can stand behind.

- **_Research your craft:_** There are webinars, classes, workshops, and seminars offered regularly on a wide array of topics. Sign up to receive daily news and updates from an informative website. Visit a bookstore or library and search for books and magazines that can help you with your business.

Chapter 5

Your marketing efforts are most effective when they are seen where your target audience can appreciate them the most. Researching your target's interests or places they regularly visit can help you understand where to spend your advertising dollars.

If you are going to get an outside team to do your marketing, be careful of who you hire to represent you and your brand. What is their experience? Who are their references? What goals are they required to reach?

Conclusion

You may have picked up this book because you are getting ready to make a change in your career and you aren't sure where to start. You may have even picked up this book because you know your business is lacking SOMETHING that is preventing it from advancing to the next level. Marketing can be the bridge that carries over brand loyalty, profit gains, and the building of partnership connections that can help you and your business to succeed. I leave you with these essentials to remember:

- Figure out what your brand or business is. You need to be confident and sure enough of what it is you want to do so that you can tell it to another person in fifteen seconds or less.

- You never know how "Hi" can turn into "I know who can help you" or "I want to buy (your product) from you." Act accordingly.

- No one is going to care more about your business than you will.
  Follow up with those you meet and create a way for people to follow up with you. If people do not trust you they are not going to invest in your brand.

People generally want to associate marketing with two things: having to spend a lot of money and the need to be outgoing in order to succeed at it.

<u>Wrong!</u>

There are highly successful people that are achieving what they want and they do not spend a lot of money nor are they naturally outgoing. We've learned how to network and market using a lean budget, attending free or inexpensive networking events, classes and engaging with your audience on various social media platforms.

Ultimately, marketing yourself and your brand starts with the belief you have in yourself and what it is you want to accomplish. Once you know what you want to do, you will then want to spend every day working to make it attainable. Then– and only then– will everything fall into place.

Glossary

Blog/Blogging A blog is an online post similar to a diary where people post their opinions or their views. To post regular blog entries to a blog platform is an act known as *blogging*

Brand When people think of you, your values and your skills these are what make your brand

Craigslist An online classified section that has various postings from those looking to either sell to you, hire you, or inform you of their services

Facebook A social media site owned by Mark Zuckerburg. Originally created for college students to keep in touch; now used to keep in touch with family, friends, celebrities and business owners

Google Plus (also Google+) A Google owned social networking site

Instant messaging The ability to send a message to someone instantly online

Marketing A method used to tell and

show others about your product and services.

Meetup.com A website that you sign on as a member and when you put in your city and interests, your homepage will prompt you of social goups and others who share your interests in your area

Skype A video calling, conferencing, and telephone service; tool for communicating with those you may not be able to meet face-to-face. Great for interviews, meetings and conference calls.

Pinterest A social media platform where you can "pin" or like visualizations of your interests. Great for visions boards and advertising your visual creation and interests.

Twitter A social media platform used to advertise what you want as long as you say it in 140 characters or less. Sometimes referred to as *microblogging*. Posts made to this site are called *tweets*. When your followers want to take your post and put it on their timeline, they will *retweet*. If they want to save your message for a later view they can mark it as a favorite. You can also send direct and private messages to your followers as long as they follow you back.

UStream A social media site that allows you to show video footage of yourself in real time to other people online that have signed up to view your *channel*.

Webinars These are web based seminars. Used for instruction and job trainings.

www.ingramcontent.com/pod-product-compliance
Lightning Source LLC
Chambersburg PA
CBHW052030290426
44112CB00014B/2456